The Next Step

A Guide to Building a Startup Financial Plan

"LUNI" LIBES

LUNARMOBISCUIT PUBLISHING

Cover Design by Michelle Fairbanks/Fresh Design
Edited by Monica Aufrecht

Published by Lunarmobiscuit Publishing

PRINT ISBN 978-0-9980-9472-4

CONTENTS

BEFORE YOU BEGIN

Key advice before you start

making up numbers

F1: NOT ACCOUNTING

No balance sheet in sight…

THIS IS NOT a book on accounting. This book will not teach you how to create a balance sheet, income statement, nor cash flow statement. If you already know how to produce or read any of those standard accounting statements, then free your mind from any new advice that may conflict with your experience. If not, then don't worry. A startup financial plan is not that complicated.

The goal of this book is to teach you how to build a startup financial plan from scratch, specific to your business. This plan will help you answer a few key questions about your business:

> Will the business ever make money?
> If so, when will the business make a profit?
> And if so, how much money will be needed
> to reach profitability?

These answers will then tell you whether your idea is worth working on and, if so, how big of a challenge you face.

Additionally, whether the plan is viable or not, you will walk away with a far better understanding of how the money flows through your proposed business and how you could change the model to improve the business.

F2: NO TEMPLATES

When you want something done right...

EVERY COMPANY IS different, and, as such, there is no single financial plan template that works across most businesses. In fact, in my experience, starting with a template required more time and effort than starting from scratch, as every template includes some assumptions and formulas that need to be changed.

Additionally, while working with hundreds of entrepreneurs on their financial plans, the biggest issue I've seen is that many of those entrepreneurs started with a template, and, because of that, they cannot explain how it works. For instance, they do not know how any given value in a spreadsheet cell is computed.

One key purpose of building a financial model is to understand how the money flows through a business, and, to do this, you need to understand how the money flows through the spreadsheet. It is much easier to understand a spreadsheet you build yourself than one that was originally created by someone else.

Finally, a financial plan can be trusted only if you know for certain that the numbers it spits out are correct. The more complex the spreadsheet, the more likely there are "bugs" in the formula or hidden assumptions that could be false. By starting from a blank sheet, you are forced to start with a simple model. This makes the results more trustworthy, since every detail is carefully thought through as you change and improve the spreadsheet.

F3: LEMONADE

When life gives you lemons...

ONE COMMON SIMPLE business is a lemonade stand. This is a business so simple, it is often run by children. This also happens to be a business complex enough to showcase the various aspects of startup financial planning. That is why I'll use a lemonade stand as our sample business in this book.

Additionally, if you have a desire to learn basic accounting, you can continue your lemonade stand experience within *The Accounting Game* by Darrel Mullis & Judith Oloff. Their book uses a lemonade business to teach you about balance sheets, income statements, and cash-flow statements.

What makes a lemonade stand a good model business is that it has a physical product, so we can learn about manufacturing (making things, such as lemonade) and inventories (storing things, such as ingredients). It is also a food business, making it a good model for restaurants or packaged goods. But, at the same time, the manufacturing process is simple and the inventories small, so, when you need to, you can ignore those aspects and focus on the service aspect of the company.

Just in case you never took the opportunity as a child to run a lemonade stand, the business is rather simple. You acquire some lemons, water, and sugar, and mix them in a pitcher. Then you set up a table by the street, draw a sign, pick a price, and sit around for a few hours, accepting money in exchange for individual glasses of lemonade. When you get bored, you pack it all up, drink the remaining lemonade, and enjoy being a child.

F4: A SPREADSHEET

Numbers, numbers everywhere…

OVER TWENTY YEARS ago, when I set out to start my first startup, I created my financial model on a piece of paper. That was back in the days of Lotus 123, before the rise of Excel, and well before you could quickly throw together a spreadsheet using Numbers on your iPad.

Here in the twenty-first century, I highly suggest you do your financial planning within a computer spreadsheet.

If spreadsheets are your least favorite of the office suite tools, don't worry. The mostly complicated formula I use in my financial plans is called SUM, and all it does is add numbers together.

My philosophy for spreadsheets is to keep them as simple as possible. I use the spreadsheet software to organize the numbers and compute the various sums, letting me focus on quickly iterating and experimenting to best understand how the business and money interact.

Lastly, do remember to **save, and save often**. Every time you make a substantial change to your plan, save it as a new spreadsheet ("version 1," "version 2," etc.). It is useful at times to go back and see the results from a previous iteration, and you can't easily do that unless you've saved it as a separate file. It is also useful at times to experiment with the business model, and that is also best done in a separate file, so it can be easily undone if the experiment fails.

In short, it is far easier to manage twenty, thirty, or fifty copies of the spreadsheet (when well named) than rely on "Undo" to undo any change you make, as you iterate.

F5: A STORY

Numbers can tell a story too...

IF YOU PLAN to raise money or recruit a team, there is one other goal of your financial plan. It needs to convince others that the business is viable, i.e., that it will ultimately make money without requiring an unreasonable amount of initial funding.

To do this, the financial plan needs to tell a good story. A **clear**, **logical**, **believable** story about your startup.

This may seem a lot to ask from a spreadsheet, as most of the stories we've read from childhood until now do not look like pages of numbers, but nonetheless, it is possible. I have told such stories myself, walking dozens of investors through my own startup financial plans.

The key is to put the items into a logical order and explain them step by step, so the story flows in a manner that others can understand, starting at assumptions and moving through to the projections.

The sample plan later in this book will demonstrate how to do this.

F6. ASSUMPTIONS

Assume a spherical cow...

A KEY PART of that storytelling is separating your **assumptions** from your conclusions. Make your assumptions easy to see and, at the same time, easy to change.

In accounting, we use spreadsheets to record events that have already happened, such as the number of products that were sold last quarter. In that case, the numbers that went into the spreadsheet were already established.

However, in a financial plan, we do not describe the past, but, rather, the future. We are creating projections about things that have not happened yet. Therefore, many of the numbers that go into the spreadsheet are educated guesses, and are likely to change.

These educated guesses are the assumptions in your plan. The estimated number of sales. The estimated size of expenses. The projected number of employees. And so on. To make it obvious which numbers are assumptions, in my spreadsheets I color all the assumptions in blue.

Everything else in the spreadsheet I leave in **black**. This means that all the rest of the numbers on the spreadsheet, those that are not blue, are values computed via formula. This includes projected values and calculations based on the assumptions.

These formulas should be as simple as possible. With only a few exceptions, **the formulas do not contain any numbers** but, instead, simply point to cells; they copy, add, subtract, multiply, or divide the contents of the cells. This is key!

For example, the formula (below) computes the total revenues (money coming in from customers). It does this by taking the number of units sold and multiplying that by the price. "Number of units sold" is an educated guess about the number of units you will sell in the future. It is an assumption, and it might be wrong. The price is also an assumption that you might decide to change later. Thus, the number of units is visible on the spreadsheet in blue, and so is the price. To calculate revenues, the formula simply multiplies them together.

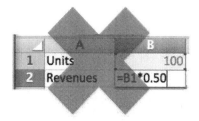

	A	B
1	Units	100
2	Revenues	=B1*0.50

	A	B
1	Units	100
2	Price	$0.50
3	Revenues	=B1*B2

This may seem simple and obvious, but many entrepreneurs I've met include numbers and prices within their formula. In practice, this makes it difficult or impossible to understand where their totals come from. You are forced to navigate through their spreadsheet, looking at every formula to find the hidden assumptions. In short, these spreadsheets fail to tell a story, since they fail to logically describe how all the assumptions fit together. Do not do this!

The one exception to this rule is formulas that deal with time. If you are converting a value from a monthly amount to an annual amount, your formula can multiple the number by twelve. If you are converting a quarterly amount to monthly, your formula can divide by three. This is because there are always three months in a quarter and twelve months in a year. These numbers are well-known and never change.

If your spreadsheet contains monthly, quarterly, and annual data (and most financial plans do), then make sure the timeframe for each value is clearly labeled.

F7: COMMAS, CURRENCY, AND PRECISION

Attention to detail is noticed, even if only unconsciously

WITH A WHOLE PAGE coated in numbers, spreadsheets can be difficult to read. To help you and your audience parse these numbers, always format the cells to include commas. For all values that display amounts of money, always include a currency symbol next to the number (e.g., "$" for dollars).

Those are two simple details that will make your spreadsheet far easier to parse and understand.

The third detail is more subtle. Spreadsheets calculate exact values. This means they are misleadingly precise. For financial plans, since all the numbers are based on guesses, exact numbers are not super important. Because of this, and also for clarity, decimals should not be shown.

For example, if the cost of your product is ten dollars, it should appear as "$10." By default, however, the spreadsheet will show this as $10.00. Luckily, you can change the formatting to show no decimal places for the numbers. The ".00" does not add anything meaningful to the spreadsheet but rather makes it harder to read and more confusing, once the values start to get large enough to include commas.

The exception is when an assumed number is between 0 and 1. For example, if one of your expenses will be fifteen cents, then it should appear as $0.15. Without decimals, this would be rounded down to $0, and that would be misleading.

Eventually, you will produce a summary of your financial plan.

Summaries do not need more than two or three "significant digits." For example, if your plan projects a value of $1,234,567, within an executive summary or slide show, round this down to $1,230,000 or more simply $1.2 million. Two or three digits of "precision" is plenty for understanding a financial model and for answering the questions about whether the company is viable.

F8: ROWS AND COLUMNS

A row is a row is a row...

SPREADSHEETS CAN BE laid out in a multitude of forms. Financial plans traditionally adhere to just one form. **Columns represent time**. Rows represent categories such as revenues, expenses, incomes, outflows, and cash.

For most financial plans, the first year is modeled monthly and subsequent years are modeled quarterly. If we follow the form, that means the first twelve columns are the first twelve months of operations. The next four columns are then the quarters of the subsequent year. And so on.

That part is simple. But, when you want to add up the numbers for the year, where do you put the total? In a column at the end of the first twelve months? Or on a different page?

There is no one right way. Instead, there are a variety of places to put annual sums. In my own financial plans and in the samples in this book, I placed the sums after the last month for the year, in their own column.

While this seems simple and it is easy to read, it does often cause problems. With this format, each row contains a mix of both values and formulas: the annual columns are computed by using a SUM formula across the month or quarter columns. Mixing values and formulas makes it difficult to cut and paste whole rows. Mixing time periods makes it complicated to turn those values into charts.

To fix these issues, some people separate out the annual sums and put them in sets of columns to the right of all others. Other people put the annual sums on a separate tab. My preference, when reading financial models, is to see the annual sums within the row next to the monthly or quarterly values, but, when creating my own models, this is the most difficult format to work with.

There is no one "best" way to format annual sums or to format any of the other details within the spreadsheet. Try a few styles to see what works best for you.

F9: ITERATION

Repeat after me... iterate, iterate, iterate.

ALL THE STEPS of business planning require iteration, and none more so than building the financial model.

The goal of the model is to understand when your company is likely to break even and how much money will be required to reach that goal. Nearly always, the first draft plan predicts that it will take far longer than you expect to reach that milestone and far more money than you have.

Even if the plan predicts that your business will do well, iterating your plan can help you find ways to succeed faster or with less initial funding. That is a win for any business!

When I have built these models myself, I have iterated through every cell in the spreadsheet at least a dozen times. Every cell. For those cells filled with potential revenues, the question to ask is, "Might this take longer than expected?" For those cells filled with expenses, the question to ask is, "Can I do without this for a month or two?" And for every cell, the question is, "Does this seem reasonable?"

When there is no more revenue to reasonably add and there are no more expenses to reasonable postpone, the financial plan is "done." Done is in quotes because it is really just done for the moment, until more information is learned and you can update, rework, and iterate once more.

FINANCIAL CONCEPTS

Key concepts to understand

before filling in the spreadsheet

F10: THE UNIT SALE

Inch, foot, fathom, mile, or parsec?

AT THE CORE of the financial plan is a concept called the "unit sale."

For most businesses, there is some packaged product or service that customers buy. For startups, there is typically just one such product or service, albeit sometimes in a few different sizes.

For example, for a car manufacturer, the unit is one car. When you go to the dealer to buy a car, you get a whole car, not an à la carte mix of three seats, five wheels, one door, half an engine, and three batteries.

For an airline, the unit is a one-way flight. I may in fact switch planes in an airport during that flight, but when I buy a ticket, I'm buying one flight from city A to city B, regardless of whether it is a direct flight or multiple hops.

For a supermarket, the unit is a "shopping cart." The transaction between market and customer involves the whole cart of items, not the individual items within the cart. The same is true for ecommerce sites, which use a virtual shopping cart.

For a magazine, the unit is an annual subscription, since, like the cart, the transaction involves the subscription, not the individual issues.

On Google, the unit is the search or the page view. In the case of Google, you and your attention are the product. The customer is the advertiser, and they purchase ad placements per search or per page.

For the lemonade stand, the unit is the glass of lemonade. Lemonade stands do not traditionally sell pitchers or bottles or six-packs or a subscription of lemonade delivered daily to your home. They sell one glass at a time.

What is the unit sale for your business?

F11: COST OF GOODS

Two steps forward, one step back...

WHAT DOES IT COST to produce one unit of production?

To answer this question, separate out all of the **variable** costs involved in creating each unit of production (a.k.a. the **cost of goods**) from the **fixed** expenses required to run your company. We deal with each of these separately.

For example, back at that car company, their cost of goods includes the costs of all the parts plus the costs of the employees working on the assembly line. The design of the car, the factory, tooling, etc. are all fixed costs that do not change when one more car is sold.

At the airline, their cost of goods is the fuel, the salaries of the crew, and the landing fees at the airports. The airplane itself is a fixed expense that does not change if one more passenger is flown.

For the supermarket, the cost of goods is the wholesale costs of the items in the cart. The building, staff, and electricity are all fixed expenses that do not change if one more customer is served.

For the magazine, the cost of goods is the price of the paper and printing costs. The salaries of the writers, photographers, and editors are all fixed expenses.

At Google, the cost of goods is too small to measure. Delivering one page of search results and delivering one set of ads for one page view costs so little, it can be ignored. Almost all of the expenses are fixed expenses. However, if Google pays its ad sales force a commission on the sale of ads, then that would be included in the cost of sales.

For our lemonade stand, the cost of goods includes the

ingredients that make up the lemonade plus the cup it is served in and the labor required to make and serve the drink. Everything else is a fixed expense.

If you are unsure about whether one of your expenses is part of the cost of goods or not, think about what happens if you make one extra unexpected sale. If that costs you a measurable amount of money, the expenses associated with that money are likely part of the cost of goods. If not, then they are a fixed expense.

Why split apart variable and fixed expense? Doing so helps you understand how your company scales. When sales double, usually cost of sales doubles as well, while fixed costs do not always go up as much. Sometimes this is obvious, like in the car company, where twice as many parts are needed.

However, also note that if car sales double, fixed costs may go up, as well, since it may not be possible to produce twice as many cars without expanding the factory that manufactures those cars.

The same is true for businesses like airlines and supermarkets and magazines. Doubling sales doubles expenses (cost of sales), but it may also require increasing fixed costs, such as adding more airplanes, more checkout lines, and more staff.

Even at companies like Google, where the cost of goods is too small to measure, doubling sales may involve more expenses, like more servers and less obvious expenses, like a larger staff that can provide more unique ads.

F12: NUMBERS OF UNITS

Two ounces, three pounds, five tons...

IT IS TIME to start predicting the future. If you have not started selling your product or service yet, this may feel like making up numbers. There is some truth in that, but if you take your time and give each number some thought, then the values you come up with will be educated guesses and will lead to useful results.

The first predictions are your **average** sale. We focus on the average because you may sell your product at different prices or may have two services, one at a low price to entice new customers and another at a high price to earn the bulk of your profits. If so, then answer the following two questions with a best guess about the average sale. If you have just one product and one price, then this is easier.

In the average sale, how many units are purchased? What is the average price per unit?

Going back to the examples, the average unit sale for a car dealer is a single car.

For airlines, the unit is the one-way flight, but the average sale contains two units, typically arranged as a round-trip flight.

At a supermarket, the average sale is one shopping cart. For a magazine, the average sale is a one-year subscription.

For Google, this question is complicated, as advertisers buy one ad at a time but typically have a monthly budget, purchasing up to a fixed amount of ads in a given month. Thus, for Google or any business like it, the second figure—average revenue per customer— is easier to predict, and the financial plan should rely more on that value than the estimated number of units.

F13: ONE GLASS OF LEMONADE

Time to get thirsty!

WITH AN UNDERSTANDING of the **unit sale** and estimates for **average sale price** and **cost of goods**, it is finally time to start creating a financial plan for our lemonade business.

The unit sale is one glass of lemonade.

The average sale is one glass with an estimated average price of $1.00.

The cost of goods include:

- 1 empty **cup**—$0.10
- 1 **lemon**, juiced—$0.25
- 1 tablespoon of **sugar**—$0.15
- 1 cup of **water**—too small to measure
- **Labor** for juicing, mixing, and serving—$0.10

The total cost of goods is estimated to be $0.60.

F14: BACK OF THE ENVELOPE

A viable plan?

BEFORE SPENDING ANY effort building a spreadsheet, I always recommend creating a "back of the envelope" calculation to quickly understand whether the business has any chance of being viable and whether, "at scale," the business looks big enough to be worth spending time on.

For the lemonade stand, we can put all the values into a table:

Example Financials: Lemonade Stand		
REVENUES		**DAY 1**
# Glasses		100
$/glass		$1.00
Gross Revenues	R1	$100.00
$/cup		$0.10
$/lemon juice		$0.25
$/sugar		$0.15
$/labor/cup		$0.10
Cost of Sales/cup		$0.60
Total Cost of Sales	R2	$60.00
TOTAL REVENUES	R	$40.00

We guessed at how many units will be sold. 100 glasses per day is a nice, round, reasonable-size number of sales that helps demonstrate how this business works.

What this calculation shows is that for every 100 glasses, the business earns a "top-line" revenue (a.k.a. "gross" revenue) of $100, but a "net revenue" of just $40. The variable expenses are sixty cents per cup. This calculation shows that for every 100 glasses, $60 of supplies and labor are needed. Like most cost of goods, most of that money is needed up front, before the business opens its doors.

If I were a child told I could make $40 selling lemonade, that would get me excited. However, if I were a sophisticated child and understood that I needed to spend $60 of my cash to make $100, earning a $40 profit, I may be far less excited.

This is important, so let me say it in another way. What we can learn from this simple back-of-the-envelope calculation is that, in this lemonade business, we need to invest $60 up front for every $100 in revenue, and of that $100, we then get our $60 back plus $40 in profits.

Compared to the stock market, that is a great investment, but only if we have $60 to invest and only if it works out as planned. In reality, two important details are missing.

First, we have not accounted for any fixed costs yet. We need a table, a pitcher, and a spoon for making and selling the lemonade. If we want to sell more than $100 in lemonade, we probably need a sign plus perhaps some flyers or other marketing materials. In any real-life company, there are quite a few of these "fixed" costs that need to be paid for before we can start selling anything.

Second, the plan may be wrong. Perhaps we'll sell just fifty glasses in a day, in which case the total revenues will be $50, the cost of goods $30, and the profits $20. Do we still want to work all day for $20 in profits? Worse, given our plan of selling 100 glasses, we may have purchased $60 worth of goods, sold only $50, and lost $10 for the day.

When putting together your back-of-the-envelope financial plan, ask yourself, "What could go wrong?"

YOUR FINANCIAL PLAN

A step-by-step guide

to create your financial plan

F15: FROM BLANK SHEET TO FINANCIAL PLAN

All journeys begin with a first step.

FINALLY, IT IS TIME to open up a blank spreadsheet and begin building an actual financial plan!

As we build this out, remember that the financial plan needs to tell a **story**. It needs to explain how and when your business will be profitable and how much investment will be needed to get there.

To ensure this story is as clear, logical, and believable as possible, we need to lay out the details in a clear and logical order. Refer to the spreadsheet at the end of this chapter as I walk you through the story.

Revenues

We begin with a time period. One month is typical. We put in two educated guesses:

- number of **units sold** in one month, and
- **price per unit**.

We then multiply these together to determine income, a.k.a. **revenues**. For the lemonade stand, to find the revenues, you multiply the number of glasses you plan to sell each month by the price per glass. The result tells us how much money we expect customers will give us. That number is called the "top-line" revenue of the business. In accounting, it is also known as "gross" revenue.

Next, we need to talk about the costs involved in making all that lemonade. How much money are we going to spend in order to give customers lemonade? From the back-of-the-envelope plan, we know that the **cost of goods per unit** includes the empty cup, one lemon, some sugar, and some labor. Add that all together to get the cost of goods for one glass of lemonade. But we plan to sell more than one glass. So, multiply the cost per glass by the total number of glasses sold to get the total cost of goods for the month.

Take the "top-line" revenue (i.e., the total amount of money you receive from your customers) and subtract the cost of goods (how much money you spend to make lemonade) to get the **net revenue**.

You spend money (cost of goods) to create and sell a product. You get money from the customer for that product (top-line revenue). After paying yourself back, the leftover money is the net revenue. You can think of the net revenues as your true income, since you had to spend money to make money.

For your business, details of your revenue will be different (unless you are also selling lemonade). Include all the important components so that anyone reviewing your plan will understand how your company earns money and how those revenues will grow as your company grows.

While filling out your spreadsheet, remember that the result is only a **financial model**. It is not reality. Models help us focus on the important details; the minor details can be left out. For example, the cost of goods in the lemonade plan does not include the water or ice or a napkin. It is assumed that these costs will be negligible; adding items to the model that do not significantly change the results is a waste of time. Such details also add a level of complexity that detracts from the storytelling.

Fixed Expenses

Moving beyond revenues, the next part of the story is about expenses. Remember, the **fixed** expenses are those costs that do not vary depending on the number of units sold.

For our lemonade business, the fixed expenses include what we pay for marketing and basic operations. The marketing expenses are further divided into signage and flyers. Operations include the cost of the table and a spoon to stir the ingredients.

For your business, there should be far more expenses, including salaries, rent, insurance, phones, Internet, postage, travel, entertainment, and so on. However, these expenses work in exactly the same way as those on the short list in the lemonade plan.

The key number for expenses is the sum of all fixed costs.

Net Profit/Loss

Once you have estimates for revenues and expenses, you have enough information to figure out if your company will make money or lose money. Making money is called making a **net profit**. Losing money is called a **net loss**. You calculate how much you make (or lose) by taking your net revenues and subtracting your expenses.

For most startups, the first month, first quarter, and first year all have net losses. For some startups, there are losses for a few years.

Remember, the key question you are trying to answer is whether your business will *ever* earn a profit. To answer this question, look at the "net profit" line in the spreadsheet. Looking into the future, does it ever become a positive number?

Investments and Loans

If you know basic accounting, then the financial plan up to this point may remind you of a "P&L," a.k.a. a profit and loss statement or an income statement. However, this is a startup financial plan, and it continues onward with a few sections that P&Ls do not typically contain.

These sections exist because we are not done telling our story. You need money to run a business. But since most startups lose money for a while, we need to explain how we will make up the difference. There are two common ways to do this: investments and loans.

The investments line is not about your company making investments. Rather, it is about other people making investments into your company. This happens when you find an investor who buys equity in your company. If you sell part of your company to an investor for $100,000, then you put the $100,000 on the **investments** line.

Or you may take out a **loan** from a bank (or friends and family) to provide money to your company, or you may use a line of credit secured by your house. Some entrepreneurs run up their credit card bills with company expenses. In all these cases, the company is borrowing the money it needs, and such money gets put on the line labeled "loans."

Additionally, you may receive grants or gifts or donations or prizes at a business plan competition, etc. This money is nice, because you do not have to pay it back. None of these are revenue, and yet it is money you can spend on your business. So you don't put these funds in the revenue section of the financial plan. Instead, you add a line down in this "Investments and Loans" section with an appropriate label.

Cash

Last but not least, we have the most important section in the whole financial plan: the line that tells us how much cash the company has.

To compute the cash, we use a formula unlike all the others in the spreadsheet. The cash value in any column (remember, columns denote time periods) is the cash from the previous time period plus the net income, investments, and loans from the current time period.

This is important, so let me explain it twice. The revenues for one time period are all listed in a single column. The total expenses for that same time period are all listed in that same single column. The net income/loss for that time period is the difference of revenues and expenses within that column. The investments and loans for that time period are again all found in that one column. Cash, however, is a running total; it takes the cash value from the previous column and adds to it the net income, investments, and loans.

The reason we compute cash in this way is because we need to know if and when the company will run out of cash. If there is no cash, then we cannot operate the business. No cash, no payroll. No payroll, no employees. No cash, no money to pay for the cost of goods. No goods, and there is nothing to sell.

If you run out of cash, your company dies and, with it, your dream.

Lemonade Stand: Financial Plan	Month 1
REVENUES	
# Glasses	
$/Glass	
Gross revenues	
$/cup	
$/lemon	
$/sugar/cup	
$/labor/cup	
Cost of sales/cup	
Cost of sales	
Net revenues	
EXPENSES	
Marketing	
Signage	
Flyers	
Operations	
Table	
Wooden spoon	
Total Expenses	
NET PROFIT/(LOSS)	
INVESTMENTS	
LOANS	
CASH	

F16: MONTH 1

WITH ALL THE categories of revenues and expenses established, it is time to begin filling out the financial plan with numbers.

For most businesses, the best practice is to create a monthly model for the first year of revenues and expenses. Twelve columns of numbers, one per month. For subsequent years, quarterly estimates are usually sufficient. Four columns, one per quarter. The best practice is to include at least three years of financial projections; at most, five.

The exception to these practices is for a business where some other time period is more important. For example, you may sell a product by the week and thus want to include weekly projections. Or your business may be based around school semesters or five events, etc. Use the time periods that make the most sense for your business.

For our lemonade business, monthly expenses works just fine. Below are the estimates for Month 1, of Year 1.

All the blue numbers are assumptions, i.e., estimates. All the black numbers are the result of a formula, adding or subtracting or multiplying the assumptions. With these numbers in place, the descriptions from the last chapter should make more sense.

The plan estimates that 1,000 glasses of lemonade will be sold at $1.00 per glass. This provides net revenues of $400, after paying for all the costs of goods. There are only $80 in fixed expenses, and thus the net income is $320 in profit. With no investments or loans, that means we will have $320 in cash to deposit into the bank at the end of the month.

Amazingly, this lemonade business is profitable. Perhaps that is why so many kids try it out. However, do note that, after a whole month of operations, those profits are only $320 or just over $10 per day, assuming the business operates every day. Profits are certainly good, but the scale of those profits is rather small.

Also note that this financial model doesn't explain where the $600 came from to buy the cups, lemons, and sugar, nor the $80 for the table, signage, flyers, and spoon. If this were your business and you didn't have $680 in savings for the startup or a lemon tree, spare table, and donated paper, you might need to break down the Month 1 model into weeks or day, to compute exactly how little money is needed before there really are profits to run the business. That is, maybe you don't need the full $680 to get started but instead need only $60 upfront, enough to buy the table, some flyers, and sufficient lemonade supplies for the first day, and then you can grow, using profits day by day, throughout the rest of the month.

For now, let's not worry about the $680 of startup costs and just enjoy looking at the $320 in cash from our profitable lemonade stand.

Lemonade Stand: Financial Plan		
		Month 1
REVENUES		
	# Glasses	1,000
	$/Glass	$1
	Gross revenues	$1,000
	$/cup	$0.10
	$/lemon	$0.25
	$/sugar/cup	$0.15
	$/labor/cup	$0.10
	Cost of sales/cup	$0.60
	Cost of sales	$600
	Net revenues	**$400**
EXPENSES		
	Marketing	$60
	Signage	$10
	Flyers	$50
	Operations	$20
	Table	$15
	Wooden spoon	$5
	Total Expenses	**$80**
NET PROFIT/(LOSS)		$320
INVESTMENTS		$0
LOANS		$0
CASH		$320

F17: MONTH 2

ONWARD TO THE second month. As you go through from month to month, spend some time looking at and thinking about your estimates. But not too much time. There will plenty of time later, as you iterate through the plan to question every value and fine-tune your estimates. It is more important in this first pass to get an initial first draft of estimates as quickly as possible, so you can prove to yourself that the business is worth pursuing.

For our lemonade business, like most businesses, there are fewer assumptions in Month 2 versus Month 1. Most of the numbers stay the same. Since the financial model is in a spreadsheet, and since we will be changing numbers later, don't copy the numeric values from Month 1 to Month 2. Instead, use a formula that copies the values for us.

For example, the "$/cup" in the cost of goods in Month 2 uses the formula "=D10," where "D10" is the name of the cell with the "$/cup" value from Month 1. With this formula, if we change the price per cup to $0.09 in Month 1, it will automatically change in Month 2.

Make sure the values computed by these (simple) formulas are colored black, since they are computed. With that coloring in place, when you see a number in black in a new column next to a number in blue in last month's column, you will instantly know that the value in black is unchanged from month to month (or quarter to quarter).

In the estimates for Month 2, we predict we will sell more glasses of lemonade, growing from 1,000 to 1,200. It is assumed that we will have the same number of employees, even with this growth in sales, and thus the cost per cup in labor goes down slightly, from $.10 per cup for labor to $.09 per cup. (The same number of people are working the same amount of time but selling more cups.)

Regarding the other fixed expenses, we don't need another table or sign or a new spoon, thus our only expense is more flyers.

With these estimates in place, the "bottom line" (another name for the net profit) is a profit of $432. What a great business!

We still haven't received any investments or loans, thus we have another $432 to deposit into our bank account. The cash line, as explained above, is the balance of this fictional bank account. It is the sum of the previous balance, $320, plus our net profit, $432, plus any investments and loans, $0; a total of $752.

At this point, you might think this is a near-perfect business. Two months of projections, and two months of profits. Before you get too excited, note there is a lot more work to do to understand how this business operates at scale.

Lemonade Stand: Financial Plan		
	Month 1	Month 2
REVENUES		
# Glasses	1,000	1,200
$/Glass	$1.00	$1.00
Gross revenues	$1,000	$1,200
$/cup	$0.10	$0.10
$/lemon	$0.25	$0.25
$/sugar/cup	$0.15	$0.15
$/labor/cup	$0.10	$0.09
Cost of sales/cup	$0.60	$0.59
Cost of sales	$600	$708
Net revenues	**$400**	**$492**
EXPENSES		
Marketing	$60	$60
Signage	$10	$0
Flyers	$50	$60
Operations	$20	$0
Table	$15	$0
Wooden spoon	$5	$0
Total Expenses	**$80**	**$60**
NET PROFIT/(LOSS)	**$320**	**$432**
INVESTMENTS	$0	$0
LOANS	$0	$0
CASH	$320	$752

F18: MONTH 3

WITH TWO MONTHS of profitable operations in hand, it is time to scale up this business.

For most businesses, it takes quite a lot longer than two months before the business is profitable or ready to be doubled in size. However, I am trying to demonstrate the common features of financial planning, thus, for Month 3, I have created the unrealistic scenario where sales more than double.

To grow sales to 2,500 glasses of lemonade, we lower the price to $0.75 per glass. We assume we can double sales without adding any staff, and thus the labor cost per glass drops in half, to $0.05 per glass.

We do assume that doubling sales will require a lot more marketing, including a professionally printed sign and professionally printed flyers. And to ensure those glasses are processed quickly, we buy a second table and a second spoon.

With the drop in price, our net revenues still grow, but only by $8 more than the previous month, to $500. With the added expenses, for the first time, our expenses exceed our revenues, and we have a loss.

Given the loss, why might this be a reasonable choice?

First and foremost, we are trying here to create a viable business. Profits are nice, but $752 in profits after two months of effort is not enough to support an American family.

Secondly, part of the losses this month were due to the $100 sign. That sign gets reused next month and every month for a few years. Thus, it is an investment. The same is true of the second table and spoon. (The accountants at this point can start complaining about capital expenses versus operational expenses and the lack of amortization, but ignore them. We are entrepreneurs, and we are modeling a business. We care only about cash.)

Lemonade Stand: Financial Plan	Month 1	Month 2	Month 3
REVENUES			
# Glasses	1,000	1,200	2,500
$/Glass	$1.00	$1.00	$0.75
Gross revenues	$1,000	$1,200	$1,875
$/cup	$0.10	$0.10	$0.10
$/lemon	$0.25	$0.25	$0.25
$/sugar/cup	$0.15	$0.15	$0.15
$/labor/cup	$0.10	$0.09	$0.05
Cost of sales/cup	$0.60	$0.59	$0.55
Cost of sales	$600	$708	$1,375
Net revenues	**$400**	**$492**	**$500**
EXPENSES			
Marketing	$60	$60	$1,100
Signage	$10	$0	$100
Flyers	$50	$60	$500
Trade Show			$500
Operations	$20	$0	$40
Table	$15	$0	$30
Wooden spoon	$5	$0	$10
Total Expenses	**$80**	**$60**	**$1,140**
NET PROFIT/(LOSS)	**$320**	**$432**	**($640)**
INVESTMENTS	$0	$0	$0
LOANS	$0	$0	$0
CASH	**$320**	**$752**	**$112**

The other lesson to learn from this month's results is that, as a business, despite the loss, we still have cash in the bank. We lost $620 of our $752, leaving us with $112.

Or, in other words, we could afford to make these investments and afford these losses. In contrast, a negative number under cash would mean that we could not afford the investments. Once you run out of cash, you can't run your business anymore, even if you have a great product and happy customers, because you cannot afford to get the product to them. Always keep your eye on your cash!

And a reminder: this is our first pass through the plan, not the last word in how we think this business should be run.

F19: MONTH 4

IN MONTH FOUR, we do not double sales… We quadruple them.

Again, this is not something that a typical startup would do in one month, but it demonstrates an important aspect of financial planning.

The only change to the revenues is increasing the number of glasses to 10,000. You can easily see that nothing else is changed, as all of the other numbers are black.

10,000 glasses in a month is an average of over 300 glasses of lemonade per day. To reasonably sell and serve that much lemonade will likely require multiple locations. With multiple locations and with a business that is earning $7,500 in top-line revenues, we need to consider having some management in this company.

To model the cost of our employees, a new subsection has been added to the expenses labeled "Salaries." The simplest way to model the cost of employees is to make assumptions about the number of employees and the average cost per employee. Then multiply those two numbers together to get the total employee expenses.

Your business may need more details than this, especially if you have a mix of full-time and part-time staff or a large staff with varying salaries or any structure more complicated than this chain of lemonade stands. However, no matter how much detail you include, the key number you must compute for employees is how much they cost in cash, which counts as another fixed cost.

Lemonade Stand: Financial Plan		Month 1	Month 2	Month 3	Month 4
REVENUES					
	# Glasses	1,000	1,200	2,500	10,000
	$/Glass	$1.00	$1.00	$0.75	$0.75
Gross revenues		$1,000	$1,200	$1,875	$7,500
	$/cup	$0.10	$0.10	$0.10	$0.10
	$/lemon	$0.25	$0.25	$0.25	$0.25
	$/sugar/cup	$0.15	$0.15	$0.15	$0.15
	$/labor/cup	$0.10	$0.09	$0.05	$0.05
	Cost of sales/cup	$0.60	$0.59	$0.55	$0.55
Cost of sales		$600	$708	$1,375	$5,500
Net revenues		$400	$492	$500	$2,000
EXPENSES					
Marketing		$60	$60	$1,100	$1,500
	Signage	$10	$0	$100	$500
	Flyers	$50	$60	$500	$1,000
	Trade Show			$500	$0
Operations		$20	$0	$40	$50
	Table	$15	$0	$30	$50
	Wooden spoon	$5	$0	$10	$0
Salaries		$0	$0	$0	$2,000
	# Employees	1	1	2	2
	Monthly Salary	$0	$0	$0	$1,000
Total Expenses		$80	$60	$1,140	$3,550
NET PROFIT/(LOSS)		$320	$432	($640)	($1,550)
INVESTMENTS		$0	$0	$0	$0
LOANS		$0	$0	$0	$0
CASH		$320	$752	$112	($1,438)

What happens to our lemonade business when we quadruple sales, add in the necessary marketing and equipment to make those sales, and start paying employees a salary? We lose money.

At the same time, however, Month 4 is the first month that this business resembles a real business rather than a hobby. If the monthly revenues continued to run like this for a whole year, the business would earn a total of $90,000 in gross revenues. This is called a "run rate," and our business has a "run rate" of $90,000 ($90,000 = $7,500 x 12). (Note, however, that the net revenue would be only $24,000 ($2,000 x 12), and that still doesn't account for fixed expenses).

The business also seems more real because it has paid employees. Those salaries, albeit small, are at least some incentive for the workers to sit around all day, mixing and pouring lemonade.

Banks do not allow a business to have a negative balance, and thus we need to do something within the model to make that cash balance positive.

On paper, this fix is simple. We find investors to invest in our company. In reality, this is itself a complex, time-consuming, often difficult process, but that is a lesson for another time. For now, we assume we can find investors whenever the need arises.

	Month 1	Month 2	Month 3	Month 4
NET PROFIT/(LOSS)	$320	$432	($640)	($1,550)
INVESTMENTS	$0	$0	$0	$2,000
LOANS	$0	$0	$0	$0
CASH	$320	$752	$112	$562

To overcome the negative cash balance of $1,438, we need to raise at least $1,500 from investors. To add a bit of "cushion," in case the reality of running the business does not match the plan, I've rounded this up to $2,000.

This $2,000 goes in the line labeled "Investments," and, with that, the month ends with a positive cash balance. (Remember that the cash balance includes the net loss plus the investments and loans.)

In addition, recall in Month 1 how the cash at the end of the month did not account for the $560 in startup costs? Similarly, it is unclear when, during Month 4, the $2,000 must arrive so there is enough cash to operate the company. If it arrives on Day 1 of Month 4, all will be well, but Day 30 is likely too late.

When implementing a financial plan, (i.e., when you are actually operating your business), it is far better to get the investments a month or two or three before the funds are needed, rather than in the month the financial plan calls for them.

Run out of cash and your company dies.

F20: MONTHS 5-12

CONTINUE FOR THE next eight months. Month by month, begin by estimating the revenues. If needed, adjust the cost of goods. Think about how the expenses change as the number of sales increase.

For Year 1, the typical pattern is that, each month, you have higher revenues and expenses, and, for most companies, you also have higher losses each month.

For this lemonade business, in Month 5, with sales growing 20% to 12,000 glasses, the losses are $600, and, despite rounding up the investment in Month 4, we run out of cash again. Thus, for Month 5, another $2,000 in investment is needed.

Note that, in the real world, when you are raising money from investors, you do not raise it in small, piecemeal amounts as needed but rather take the sum of all the investment needs, round that up, and aim to raise it all before any investment is needed. For this lemonade business, that means adding the $2,000 from Month 4 to the $2,000 from Month 5, rounding it up to $5,000, and aiming to raise it during Month 3.

Moving on. In Month 6, sales grow 25% to 15,000 glasses, and, due to the addition of a third employee, the losses do not just continue, they grow. However, like in Month 3, we still have enough cash in the bank to absorb those losses, thus no additional investment is needed.

In Month 7, sales grow to 20,000 glasses (double from Month 4), and we have one loss before "turning the corner" and seeing profits in every month for the remainder of the year. We are short only $100 in cash for that month, thus, rather than finding another investor, we turn to a friend and borrow $500.

Since this $500 is a loan, it goes on the line labeled "loans." When the money comes in, I color it green. When we start paying back the loan, I color the cell red. In Month 8, we pay back $100 of the loan. In Months 9, we pay back $200, and by Month 10, we plan to finish paying off the loan. Since our friend asks for no interest for this very short-term, three-month loan, we simply show a monthly repayment of $100 or $200 on that same line in the model, and each repayment is a negative number (which appears in red in my spreadsheet).

If you take out a bank loan instead of asking a friend, you might add two more lines to your financial model: one for repayment of the principal, and another for the interest expenses. Same thing for using a line of credit or credit card.

Back to the lemonade business. Months 8, 9, 10, 11, and 12 continue to grow sales, and each month increases the expenses to match the increased level of sales.

By the time we get to Month 12, this business is projected to sell 100,000 glasses of lemonade, earning $75,000 in revenues with a staff of seven, a monthly net profit of $10,780, and $21,012 in cash in the bank.

That is quite a change from the $320 profit in Month 1.

Is this plan realistic? Can you imagine selling 100,000 glasses of lemonade? Is a staff of seven people big enough to do that? Has enough been spent on marketing to drive that level of business? Or too much? What other expenses are missing?

These are the types of questions you should be asking about this plan, and you should ask the same questions about your own plan.

Lemonade Stand: Financial Plan

	Month 1	Month 2	Month 3	Month 4	Month 5	Month 6	Month 7	Month 8	Month 9	Month 10	Month 11	Month 12
REVENUES												
# Glasses	1,000	1,200	2,500	10,000	12,000	15,000	20,000	25,000	35,000	50,000	75,000	100,000
$/Glass	$1.00	$1.00	$0.75	$0.75	$0.75	$0.75	$0.75	$0.75	$0.75	$0.75	$0.75	$0.75
Gross revenues	$1,000	$1,200	$1,875	$7,500	$9,000	$11,250	$15,000	$18,750	$26,250	$37,500	$56,250	$75,000
$/cup	$0.10	$0.10	$0.10	$0.10	$0.10	$0.10	$0.10	$0.10	$0.10	$0.10	$0.10	$0.10
$/lemon	$0.25	$0.25	$0.25	$0.25	$0.25	$0.25	$0.25	$0.25	$0.25	$0.25	$0.25	$0.25
$/sugar/cup	$0.15	$0.15	$0.15	$0.15	$0.15	$0.15	$0.15	$0.15	$0.15	$0.15	$0.15	$0.15
$/labor/cup	$0.10	$0.09	$0.05	$0.05	$0.06	$0.05	$0.05	$0.05	$0.05	$0.06	$0.05	$0.05
Cost of sales/cup	$0.60	$0.59	$0.55	$0.55	$0.55	$0.55	$0.55	$0.55	$0.55	$0.55	$0.55	$0.55
Cost of sales	$600	$708	$1,375	$5,500	$6,600	$8,250	$11,000	$13,750	$19,250	$27,500	$41,250	$55,000
Net revenues	$400	$492	$500	$2,000	$2,400	$3,000	$4,000	$5,000	$7,000	$10,000	$15,000	$20,000
EXPENSES												
Marketing	$60	$60	$1,100	$1,500	$1,000	$1,100	$1,700	$1,400	$2,100	$1,800	$2,750	$2,000
Signage	$10	$0	$100	$500	$0	$0	$500	$0	$500	$0	$750	$0
Flyers	$50	$60	$500	$1,000	$1,000	$1,100	$1,200	$1,400	$1,600	$1,800	$2,000	$2,000
Trade Show	$0	$0	$500	$0	$0	$0	$0	$0	$0	$0	$0	$0
Operations	$20	$0	$40	$50	$60	$60	$110	$110	$160	$160	$220	$220
Table	$15	$0	$30	$50	$50	$50	$100	$100	$150	$150	$200	$200
Wooden spoon	$5	$0	$10	$0	$10	$10	$10	$10	$10	$10	$20	$20
Salaries	$0	$0	$0	$2,000	$2,000	$3,000	$3,000	$3,000	$4,000	$5,000	$6,000	$7,000
# Employees	1	1	2	2	2	3	3	3	4	5	6	7
Monthly Salary	$0	$0	$0	$1,000	$1,000	$1,000	$1,000	$1,000	$1,000	$1,000	$1,000	$1,000
Total Expenses	$80	$60	$1,140	$3,550	$3,060	$4,160	$4,810	$4,510	$6,260	$6,960	$8,970	$9,220
NET PROFIT/(LOSS)	$320	$432	($640)	($1,550)	($660)	($1,160)	($810)	$490	$740	$3,040	$6,030	$10,780
INVESTMENTS	$0	$0	$0	$2,000	$2,000	$0	$0	$0	$0	$0	$0	$0
LOANS	$0	$0	$0	$0	$0	$0	$500	($100)	($200)	($200)	$0	$0
CASH	$320	$752	$112	$562	$1,902	$742	$432	$822	$1,362	$4,202	$10,232	$21,012

F21: VISUALIZATION

I AM A VISUAL thinker. I am able to understanding what a given number means when analyzing a spreadsheet, but I cannot easily visualize whether the numbers as a whole are a good story or not.

However, since a financial plan is a "time series" of values, those values can easily be plotted on a chart, and a chart lets me quickly determine whether a financial plan is reasonable or not.

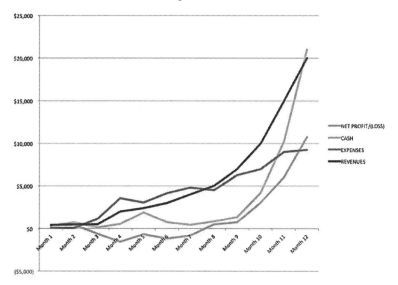

The above *Financial Summary Chart* visualizes the lemonade financial plan, with the revenues, expenses, net profit/loss, and cash as separate lines. Here is what I see within this chart.

Revenues are steadily growing, projected into a very smooth exponential curve. Real-world revenues are rarely that smooth, but this is what you are aiming for. For a financial plan, this is a good shape for Year 1, with no abrupt changes that would need further explanation.

Expenses are bumpier but not too bumpy. Expenses tend to be less smooth, as they include investments, which can make the graph spike upwards.

To see if a company is viable, look at where the revenues cross over the expenses. Since most companies lose money for a while, the expenses will start out higher than the revenues. To make money, the revenues must grow faster than expenses grow; at some point, those two lines cross.

In this chart, that crossover is clearly visible in Month 8. The same information is also visible from the net profit/loss line, which dips below the $0 mark (meaning losses), and then pops back to positive (profits) in Month 8.

Looking further at the net losses, note how shallow that dip below $0 is, as compared with the revenues and expenses. If this were a business that required a lot more upfront expenses, the net loss line would drop much lower.

What I also see from the net profit/loss line is that this business runs near break-even until Month 10, and then the profits take off dramatically. That makes me wonder how it might be possible to speed up that initial period of growth to less than ten months, in order to make the plan better. It also makes me wonder what happens in Month 10 of the plan that might not happen in reality. For example, it may be that the expenses are accurately estimated for the first nine months and then underestimated beyond that.

Lastly, let's look at the line that charts the cash on hand. **The key is that this line can never go below $0, because that would mean the company runs out of cash.** With this chart, I can see clearly how the financial plan has no cushion for nine months. Thus, in reality, if the revenues do not "meet the projections" (i.e., they fall short) or if the expenses are higher than expected, this business will likely run out of cash. That would be bad. Remember, if you run out of cash, your company dies.

F22: YEAR 1

WITH TWELVE MONTHS of a financial plan on the spreadsheet, the next step is to create an annualized summary for Year 1.

There are quite a few ways to organize annual summaries with no one best way.

My favorite way uses a feature within Excel called "Groups." In my version of Excel, this can be found on the "Data" ribbon. This grouping function allows a series of columns to be hidden (and unhidden) by clicking a control that appears above the rightmost column. (This feature can be seen in the spreadsheet below as the box above column P.)

This grouping function allows a series of columns to be hidden (and unhidden) by clicking a control that appears above the rightmost column.

When using this feature, the annual summary is always shown, and the monthly or quarterly data can be hidden away until such details are needed.

When creating an annual summary, pay attention to which rows have values that can be summed into a total. For some rows, summing up the values would make no sense. For example, you can sum the number of glasses and sum the revenues to create totals for the year, but the sum of the price of sugar is meaningless.

In the lemonade plan, all the rows where totals make sense use the SUM formula to create the annual total from the monthly data. To make it clear that these values are sums, I format them as bold.

Do note that the cash line *should not be summed*, since it is a running total for the month! The cash for the year is just the ending cash for Month 12. Since cash is such an important metric in the financial plan, I include a double-checked value in this spreadsheet. This is the small, gray value underneath the cash line for Year 1. It is the same formula used in Month 1. Take the net profit/loss for the year, and add the investment and loans to it.

With these annual totals, it is much clearer how big this lemonade business is expected to be by the end of the first year. Almost 350,000 glasses of lemonade sold. Over $250,000 dollars in "gross" revenues. $52,000 in expenses. All on just $4,000 in investments, plus a small loan that was paid off so quickly, it does not even appear in the annual summary.

Once you have the first annual summary for your business, it is time to look through the values again and question whether they look reasonable. If the revenues seem high, go back month by month and lower the projections. If the expenses seem low, go back and find the right time to add in enough expenses to justify your revenues.

For the lemonade plan, it seems unlikely that $16,000 in marketing will drive $250,000 in sales. It seems even more unlikely that a business generating $250,000 in sales would pay only $35,000 in total salaries for the year. The number of employees needed and salaries for those employees is probably underestimated.

Lemonade Stand: Financial Plan

	Month 1	Month 2	Month 3	Month 4	Month 5	Month 6	Month 7	Month 8	Month 9	Month 10	Month 11	Month 12	Year 1
REVENUES													
# Glasses	1,000	1,200	2,500	10,000	12,000	15,000	20,000	25,000	35,000	50,000	75,000	100,000	346,700
$/Glass	$1.00	$1.00	$0.75	$0.75	$0.75	$0.75	$0.75	$0.75	$0.75	$0.75	$0.75	$0.75	
Gross revenues	$1,000	$1,200	$1,875	$7,500	$9,000	$11,250	$15,000	$18,750	$26,250	$37,500	$56,250	$75,000	$260,575
$/cup	$0.10	$0.10	$0.10	$0.10	$0.10	$0.10	$0.10	$0.10	$0.10	$0.10	$0.10	$0.10	
$/lemon	$0.25	$0.25	$0.25	$0.25	$0.25	$0.25	$0.25	$0.25	$0.25	$0.25	$0.25	$0.25	
$/sugar/cup	$0.15	$0.15	$0.15	$0.15	$0.15	$0.15	$0.15	$0.15	$0.15	$0.15	$0.15	$0.15	
$/labor/cup	$0.10	$0.09	$0.05	$0.05	$0.05	$0.05	$0.05	$0.05	$0.05	$0.05	$0.05	$0.05	
Cost of sales/cup	$0.60	$0.59	$0.55	$0.55	$0.55	$0.55	$0.55	$0.55	$0.55	$0.55	$0.55	$0.55	
Cost of sales	$600	$708	$1,375	$5,500	$6,600	$8,250	$11,000	$13,750	$19,250	$27,500	$41,250	$55,000	$190,783
Net revenues	$400	$492	$500	$2,000	$2,400	$3,000	$4,000	$5,000	$7,000	$10,000	$15,000	$20,000	$69,792
EXPENSES													
Marketing	$60	$60	$1,100	$1,500	$1,000	$1,100	$1,700	$1,400	$2,100	$1,800	$2,750	$2,000	$16,570
Signage	$10	$0	$100	$500	$0	$0	$500	$0	$500	$0	$750	$0	
Flyers	$50	$60	$500	$1,000	$1,000	$1,100	$1,200	$1,400	$1,600	$1,800	$2,000	$2,000	
Trade Show	$0	$0	$500	$0	$0	$0	$0	$0	$0	$0	$0	$0	
Operations	$20	$0	$40	$50	$60	$60	$110	$110	$160	$160	$220	$220	$1,210
Table	$15	$0	$30	$50	$50	$50	$100	$100	$150	$150	$200	$200	
Wooden spoon	$5	$0	$10	$0	$10	$10	$10	$10	$10	$10	$20	$20	
Salaries	$0	$0	$0	$2,000	$2,000	$3,000	$3,000	$3,000	$4,000	$5,000	$6,000	$7,000	$35,000
# Employees	1	1		2	2	3	3	3	4	5	6	7	
Monthly Salary	$0	$0	$0	$1,000	$1,000	$1,000	$1,000	$1,000	$1,000	$1,000	$1,000	$1,000	
Total Expenses	$80	$60	$1,140	$3,550	$3,060	$4,160	$4,810	$4,510	$6,260	$6,960	$8,970	$9,220	$52,780
NET PROFIT/(LOSS)	$320	$432	($640)	($1,550)	($660)	($1,160)	($810)	$490	$740	$3,040	$6,030	$10,780	$17,012
INVESTMENTS	$0	$0	$0	$2,000	$2,000	$0	$0	$0	$0	($200)	$0	$0	$4,000
LOANS	$0	$0	$0	$0	$0	$500	$500	($100)	($200)	$0	$0	$0	$0
CASH	$320	$752	$112	$562	$1,902	$742	$432	$822	$1,363	$4,202	$10,232	$21,012	$21,012
													$21,012

F23: YEAR 2

NEXT, REPEAT YOUR projections for Year 2. For most businesses, it is sufficient to use quarterly projections/estimates after Year 1, rather than stick with monthly.

Quarterly is usually sufficient for two reasons. First, the uncertainty of your estimates increases the longer into the future you try to predict. Thus, whether an expense will be needed in February or March of next year is hard to predict with any accuracy. Knowing whether it will be in the first quarter or the third quarter is good enough. Second, many businesses have seasonal changes, and quarterly values make those ups and downs more obvious. For example, if we assume this lemonade business is running in a temperate climate in the northern hemisphere, then it is likely that sales will be largest in the third quarter, during the summer, and lowest in the midst of winter, which is the first quarter.

This type of seasonality is demonstrated in Year 2 of the lemonade financial plan. Q1 drops total quarterly sales below that of Month 12 and, to match that drop in revenue, lowers all marketing and operational expenses to zero. Despite the lowered expenses, the quarter has a net loss.

Sales are then projected to grow in Q2 and Q3, returning the company to profitability, until Q4, when it once again loses money.

Looking at the annual summary, we see that the total sales are projected to rise to over 1,000,000 glasses of lemonade, just shy of triple the Year 1 results. Upon reflection, this seems unlikely without tripling the marketing budget or tripling the staff, but we will get back to that after we have three years of estimates entered into the plan.

	Q1	Q2	Q3	Q4	Year 2
REVENUES					
# Glasses	60,000	300,000	400,000	250,000	**1,010,000**
$/Glass	$0.75	$0.75	$0.75	$0.75	
Gross revenues	$45,000	$225,000	$300,000	$187,500	**$757,500**
$/cup	$0.10	$0.10	$0.10	$0.10	
$/lemon	$0.28	$0.28	$0.28	$0.28	
$/sugar/cup	$0.17	$0.17	$0.17	$0.17	
$/labor/cup	$0.05	$0.05	$0.05	$0.05	
Cost of sales/cup	$0.60	$0.60	$0.60	$0.60	
Cost of sales	$36,000	$180,000	$240,000	$150,000	**$606,000**
Net revenues	$9,000	$45,000	$60,000	$37,500	**$151,500**
					$151,500
EXPENSES					
Marketing	$0	$2,500	$3,000	$3,500	**$9,000**
Signage	$0	$0	$0	$0	
Flyers	$0	$2,000	$2,000	$2,000	
Trade Show	$0	$500	$1,000	$1,500	
Operations	$0	$330	$330	$330	**$990**
Table	$0	$300	$300	$300	
Wooden spoon	$0	$30	$30	$30	
Salaries	$25,200	$28,800	$32,400	$36,000	**$122,400**
# Employees	7	8	9	10	
M/Q Salary	$1,200	$1,200	$1,200	$1,200	
Total Expenses	$25,200	$31,630	$35,730	$39,830	**$132,390**
NET PROFIT/(LOSS)	($16,200)	$13,370	$24,270	($2,330)	**$19,110**
INVESTMENTS	$0	$0	$0	$0	**$0**
LOANS	$0	$0	$0	$0	**$0**
CASH	$4,812	$18,182	$42,452	$40,122	**$40,122**

Lemonade Stand: Financial

F24: YEAR 3

NEXT, WE FILL OUT the projections for Year 3. For the lemonade plan, three years is sufficient. For your business, if you can predict out five years, then keep going and add Years 4 and 5.

For this lemonade plan, Year 3 looks a lot like Year 2. Total sales are projected to grow 25%, and the expenses are modified to match.

Year 3 again includes the seasonable nature of the business, with one new idea in the model. We now adjust the number of employees according to the season.

Looking at the annual summaries, the most unbelievable part of Year 3 is that the total expenses for marketing and operations are unchanged from Year 2. Comparing the quarterly values for the two years, it becomes clear that Year 3 is just a copy of Year 2.

It is in fact easiest to add each subsequent year to the financial plan by coping the columns of one year to create the next year. If you do this, do make sure you go back row by row and cell by cell to update the values so they match the expected growth in the new year.

A B	C	V	W	X	Y	Z
Lemonade Stand: Financic						
		Q1	Q2	Q3	Q4	Year 3
REVENUES						
	# Glasses	80,000	400,000	500,000	280,000	**1,260,000**
	$/Glass	$0.75	$0.75	$0.75	$0.75	
	Gross revenues	$60,000	$300,000	$375,000	$210,000	**$945,000**
	$/cup	$0.10	$0.10	$0.10	$0.10	
	$/lemon	$0.30	$0.30	$0.30	$0.30	
	$/sugar/cup	$0.20	$0.20	$0.20	$0.20	
	$/labor/cup	$0.05	$0.05	$0.05	$0.05	
	Cost of sales/cup	$0.65	$0.65	$0.65	$0.65	
	Cost of sales	$52,000	$260,000	$325,000	$182,000	**$819,000**
	Net revenues	**$8,000**	**$40,000**	**$50,000**	**$28,000**	**$126,000**
						$126,000
EXPENSES						
	Marketing	$0	$2,500	$3,000	$3,500	**$9,000**
	Signage	$0	$0	$0	$0	
	Flyers	$0	$2,000	$2,000	$2,000	
	Trade Show	$0	$500	$1,000	$1,500	
	Operations	$0	$330	$330	$330	**$990**
	Table	$0	$300	$300	$300	
	Wooden spoon	$0	$30	$30	$30	
	Salaries	$28,350	$32,400	$45,000	$28,350	**$134,100**
	# Employees	7	8	10	7	
	M/Q Salary	$1,350	$1,350	$1,500	$1,350	
	Total Expenses	**$28,350**	**$35,230**	**$48,330**	**$32,180**	**$144,090**
NET PROFIT/(LOSS)		($20,350)	$4,770	$1,670	($4,180)	($18,090)
INVESTMENTS		$0	$0	$0	$0	**$0**
LOANS		$0	$0	$0	$0	**$0**
CASH		$19,772	$24,542	$26,212	$22,032	**$22,032**
						$22,032

F25: ITERATE... ITERATE... ITERATE.

AT THIS POINT, step back and celebrate that the lemonade business has a three-year financial plan. If you have followed along in these steps with your own business, then you, too, have a first-draft financial plan.

I hate to tell you, but that was the easy part of financial planning. The difficult part comes next: iterating back through the spreadsheet, making the estimates more accurate and the resulting values more believable.

There is no shortcut to that process.

Expect to iterate at least a dozen times through the whole spreadsheet.

For each month and quarter, ask yourself, "Is it reasonable that my business will earn this much revenue?" Once you believe the value, go through each of the expenses and ask, "Are these expenses high enough to bring in those revenues?"

When you are happy with the monthly and quarterly numbers, look at the annual summaries, and ask the same questions again. Since the annual numbers are sums, the only fix for those numbers is back in the monthly and quarterly values. And so on and so on, until there is no revenue left to remove and no expenses left to add.

At this point, double check that your cash balance never drops below zero. When it does (and it usually does), add in enough investments to make the balance positive.

Investment

With that exercise complete, now look at the annual totals for investments. Is that an amount you have in your savings account? Is it an amount you can borrow from friends and family? Is it an amount you could pitch to investors and expect to raise? And, most importantly, is that number a reasonable amount to invest, given the profits you expect to generate in Year 3? (If you are not yet profitable in Year 3 or, at worst Year 5, reconsider whether this business is worth pursuing.)

Too often, the answer to all these questions is "no."

Quite often, I meet entrepreneurs who share plans with me that require $500,000 in investments but only generate $500,000 in revenues by Year 3. Those revenues are not large enough to pay back the investors with a reasonable return, and thus the "ask" of investors is simply too large.

And even if the numbers look good, it is still challenging to find investors. Maybe you can run your business without them.

Make a copy of your plan. Now change the numbers to see if you can reduce the amount of money needed from investors. Can you get that number low enough that you can give your company the needed cash from your own savings and skip investors completely? If so, you might be able to bootstrap your company.

"Bootstrapping" means paying for the startup costs yourself, instead of with investments. Most startups are bootstrapped, which means they are funded by the founder, their friends and family, and, these days, $5,000-$25,000 in crowdfunding. Can you make your plan profitable on that?

If not profitable, can you at least create a company with meaningful revenues? If you cannot run your business without investors, maybe you can at least get it started. You will have a far easier time raising money from investors with a revenue-generating company already running than with just a business plan on a piece of paper, no matter how compelling the financials appear to be.

Stress

Lastly, take this opportunity of iteration to "stress" your plan, to understand what might happen once you start the company.

Drop the revenues in half. How does that impact the time until the company becomes "cash flow positive," i.e., when the net losses turn into net profits? How does it change the total investment dollars needed?

Add more staff. It is difficult to imagine how many people are required to sell $1,000,000 worth of products and services and to support those customers, keep up with the marketing, do the accounting, etc. For many companies, the biggest expenses are the people. Add a few extra people into the plan, and see what happens.

Delay the first outside investment by three months. Raising money is difficult. Most companies that try never even get an investment. Push back your investment by three months, adjust the plan so you do not run out of cash, and see the results. Is the business still worth doing?

Now push the investment out six months. Is the business still worth launching?

Mix all these scenarios together and you will have a more realistic plan. Sales will likely be slower than you expect. Expenses will likely be higher than you expect. Investments will likely take longer than you expect. If you have a plan that anticipates these common outcomes and that plan is still viable, (i.e., it is worth investing your time and effort), then you are in much better shape than the previous iteration, which lacked these reality-checks.

"Done"

At some point, you have a plan that has been iterated so many times, you can't find anything reasonable to change. At that point, you are done. For now.

With that, it is time to ask the key questions:

Is that plan viable?
Does it make a profit?
When and how much?
How much money is needed?
How many people are needed?

After sleeping on this "final" financial plan, with the answers to these questions in hand, do you still think this business is a good idea?

Does your partner agree? Does your spouse agree?

Either way, congratulations. Either way, you should now know far better how your business actually works, at least in terms of revenue, expenses, and investments.

But do note that you are never truly done with this plan. Because..., as soon as you launch your product, you'll learn more about your market than you know now. With that knowledge, you will realize that your financial plan is wrong. You will have discovered that a financial plan is never done and it is simply time for the next iteration...

EXTRA

THE NEXT STEP provides a set of frameworks for building a business plan. If you can quickly build a plan using a second framework, you should do that, too. That effort will not only give you new insights into your business, it will provide a double-check on the results of the first framework.

The following are bits of advice that provide two alternative frameworks that might be useful to your business.

X1: CUSTOMER LIFETIME VALUE

How much, how long, and how often?

FINDING CUSTOMERS costs money. How much money? Add up the cost of your marketing and pre-sales efforts. Divide that total by the number of paying customers to find your average "customer acquisition cost." For many businesses, that is a key metric to measure and manage.

For a business to be profitable, the calculation is simple: the revenue you earn from a customer must be larger than the cost of getting that customer (on average).

The tricky part comes in determining how much you earn, on average, from each customer, for as long as they are your customer. In the simplest case, your customers buy your product then never come back to buy anything again. In that case, the "lifetime value" of that customer is the revenue associated with that sale. However, if some of your customers will be repeat buyers, this can get complicated.

In the most complicated form, you sell a subscription service, with customers paying you on a periodic basis. The question is then to estimate how long, on average, that recurring revenue will last. Or, flipping that questions around, what percentage of customers will cancel their subscription in any given week/month/year?

This percentage of cancellations is called "churn," and for businesses with recurring revenues, churn is another metric to measure and minimize.

In all cases, from simple to complex, understanding the lifetime value of your customer will help you plan and manage your pre-sales and post-sales efforts.

In your planning, just like with other assumptions in your financial plan, make your best guess on these values. Then measure and iterate that assumption as you make and eventually lose customers during the first few years of business.

X2: SCENARIO PLANNING

Given $X, how will you spend it?

THE FULL FINANCIAL plan described in the FINANCIALS section is exceedingly useful but is cumbersome and complex when it comes to answering the question:

How will you spend $X if invested?

For every business expecting to raise capital early in the business, this is a very common question. Investors look at your financial plan, see that you *need* $X, and assume that your business plan is not viable if you raise a dollar less than $X. Meanwhile, the reality is that, although you iterated and iterated the plan until it needed only $X, you can often make it work with far less, if you have to.

One solution is to build multiple versions of your financial plan to match various amounts of investments. The difficulty of doing that is the financial plan we created in the main part of this book flows from revenues and expenses down to investment needs, not the other way around.

What you need is an alternative financial plan that begins with the investment amount at the top. Such a form of plan exists. It is called a scenario plan, or often just called a "budget".

Below is a one-year budget for the lemonade business from the section on FINANCIALS. If you read that section through the first year, the categories and numbers should look familiar.

Lemonade Stand: Budget		Low	Med	High
INVESTMENT				
	Equity	**$1,000**	**$2,000**	**$4,000**
EXPENSES				
	Marketing	**$9,200**	**$10,450**	**$16,570**
	Signage	$1,500	$1,750	$2,360
	Flyers	$7,500	$8,500	$13,710
	Trade Show	$200	$200	$500
	Operations	**$825**	**$940**	**$1,210**
	Table	$750	$850	$1,095
	Wooden spoon	$75	$90	$115
	Salaries	**$15,000**	**$25,000**	**$35,000**
	EOY Employees	3	5	7
	Monthly Salary	$1,000	$1,000	$1,000
	Total Expenses	**$25,025**	**$36,390**	**$52,780**
REVENUES				
	# Glasses	**150,000**	**200,000**	**300,000**
	$/Glass	$0.75	$0.75	$0.75
	Gross revenues	**$112,500**	**$150,000**	**$225,000**
	$/cup	$0.10	$0.10	$0.10
	$/lemon	$0.25	$0.25	$0.25
	$/sugar/cup	$0.15	$0.15	$0.15
	$/labor/cup	$0.08	$0.06	$0.05
	Cost of sales/cup	$0.58	$0.56	$0.55
	Cost of sales	**$87,000**	**$112,000**	**$165,000**
	Net revenues	**$25,500**	**$38,000**	**$60,000**
NET PROFIT/(LOSS)		**$475**	**$1,610**	**$7,220**

In a budget, the investment is the top-line value, followed by the expenses then revenue and, finally, the net income. The sample budget includes three columns, each with a different amount of investment. Each investment has a different projection for expenses and revenues.

The key to budgeting is that, at each level of investment, you always set the net revenues to be positive, making whatever other adjustments are necessary. The whole point is to show how the funds will be spent and that, no matter the level of investment, the financial plan is viable.

In "real world" budgets from the companies I've advised, the first year often includes minimal revenues. In those cases, the budget is far more of a demonstration of the "use of funds.." Such budgets directly answer the question at the start of this chapter, "How will the investment be spent?" In these budgets, many of the expenses are left blank in the first and second columns, explicitly showing equipment, marketing efforts, and other expenses that would be nice to have, but which are not affordable, given a smaller amount of funding.

You can think of this from the perspective of the investor. The product your investor is buying is your company. The investor thus wants to know what they are getting for their money. What they want is not only a percentage of ownership in the company as-is, but, more importantly, they want to see your company grow in scale. Thus, they want to know how you are going to use their cash to grow your company.

A budget is a direct answer to that question.

APPENDIX

FURTHER READING

Online classes, more books, and more advice

lunarmobiscuit.com

More books in The Next Step series

The Next Step: *Guiding You From Idea to Startup*
The Next Step: *A Guide to Startup Sales and Marketing*
The Next Step: *A Guide to Pitching Your Idea*
The Next Step: *A Guide to Dividing Equity*
The Next Step: *The Realities of Funding a Startup*

Other recommended books

The Art of the Start by Guy Kawasaki
Business Model Generation by Alexander Osterwalder & Yves
     Pigneur
Crossing the Chasm by Geoffrey Moore
*The Dip: A Little Book That Teaches You When to Quit (and When to
     Stick)* by Seth Godin
Evil Plans by Hugh MacLeod
Four Steps to an Epiphany by Steve Blank
Free by Chris Anderson
Getting to Plan B, John Mullins and Randy Komisar
The Innovator's Dilemma by Clayton Christensen
Lean Startup by Eric Reis
The Monk and the Riddle by Randy Komisar

Plan B: How to Hatch a Second Plan That's Always Better Than Your First by David Murray

Purple Cow: Transform Your Business by Being Remarkable by Seth Godin

Venture Deals: Be Smarter Than Your Lawyer and Venture Capitalist by Brad Feld and Jason Mendelson

For Information on U.S. Patents and Trademarks

http://uspto.gov

ACKNOWLEDGMENTS

THANK YOU TO Gifford Pinchot III, Intrapreneur in Residence and co-founder of Pinchot University (pinchot.edu) for his foresight into the future of entrepreneurship, and his openness to my mind's wanderings.

Thank you to the staff, fellow Entrepreneurs in Residence, and researchers at the University of Washington's CoMotion center for impact and innovation (_comotion.uw.edu_), for all your feedback.

Thank you to the team at Impact Hub Seattle (impacthubseattle.com), who have created a true community space that brings together hundreds of impactful entrepreneurs.

Thank you to the "fledglings" of Fledge, the conscious company accelerator (fledge.co), and participants of Kick, "our" incubator (kickincubator.com), whose questions on entrepreneurship repeatedly demonstrate the complexity of turning ideas into startups.

And, most of all, thanks to my brilliant wife and editor, Monica Aufrecht, who relentlessly ensured my words matched my thoughts and that those words would be understandable to you, without the aid of a business school education or a business jargon dictionary.

ABOUT THE AUTHOR

MICHAEL "LUNI" LIBES is a twenty-plus-year serial entrepreneur, most recently founding Fledge LLC, the conscious company accelerator. Fledge helps entrepreneurs who aim to do good for the world while simultaneously doing good business.

fledge.co @FledgeLLC

Luni is the creator and Global Managing Director of Kick, a pre-accelerator program providing business education and guidance to entrepreneurs globally, operating in dozens of cities around the world.

kickincubator.com @KickIncubator

Luni is an Entrepreneur in Residence and Entrepreneurship Instructor at Pinchot University, advisor to The Impact Hub Seattle, to SURF Incubator, and to a dozen startup companies. He is also an Entrepreneur in Residence Emeritus for the University of Washington's CoMotion center for impact and innovation.

pinchot.edu
comotion.uw.edu
thehubseattle.com
surfincubator.com

Luni began his career in software, founding and co-founding four startups and joining a fifth. These include: Ground Truth (mobile market research and analysis), Medio Systems (mobile search and advertising), Mforma (mobile gaming and applications), 2WAY (enterprise collaboration systems), and Nimble (pen computing, PDAs, and early smartphones).

This book, the whole *Next Step* series of book, Luni's online classes, and other writing can be found at lunarmobiscuit.com. *@Lunarmobiscuit.*

INDEX